16

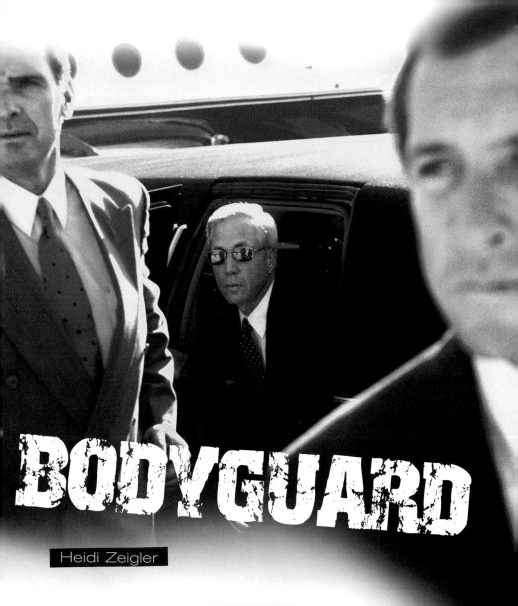

BODYGUARD

Heidi Zeigler

HIGH
interest
books

Children's Press®
A Division of Scholastic Inc.
New York / Toronto / London / Auckland / Sydney
Mexico City / New Delhi / Hong Kong
Danbury, Connecticut

Book Design: Michelle Innes and Mindy Liu
Contributing Editor: Eric Fein

Photo Credits: Cover, pp. 1, 35, 38, 40 © SuperStock, Inc.; pp. 3, 8, 29, 32, 43,
45, 47 © PictureQuest; p. 5 © Corbis; p. 10 © Szenes Jason/Corbis Sygma;
p. 7 © Micheal Krasowitz/Getty Images; pp. 9, 19, 30 © AFP/Corbis; p. 12
© Historical Picture Archive/Corbis; p. 15 © Action Plus/Icon SMI; p. 16
© Corbis Sygma; p. 21 © Mark Peterson/Corbis Sygma; p. 22 © Steve Krongard
Inc./Getty Images; pp. 24–25 © Anna Clopet/Corbis; p. 26 © David Leach/Getty
Images, Inc.; p. 36 © Getty Images

Library of Congress Cataloging-in-Publication Data

Zeigler, Heidi.
  Bodyguard / Heidi Zeigler.
  p. cm. —(Danger is my business)
  Summary: Introduces the type of work, dangers, and requirements for the
  job of bodyguard.
  Includes bibliographical references and index.
  ISBN 0-516-24341-1 (lib. bdg.)—ISBN 0-516-27863-0 (pbk.)
  1. Bodyguards—Juvenile literature. 2. Bodyguards—United
  States—Juvenile literature. [1. Bodyguards. 2. Vocational guidance.]
  I. Title. II. Series.

HV8290.Z45 2003
363.28'9—dc21
                                                      2003000783

CONTENTS

The backstage exit of the concert hall is packed with people. Some are photographers trying to snap photos of your client, a rock singer. Others are fans who want the singer to sign autographs. The crowd pushes forward. Your fellow bodyguards push the crowd back. They clear a path to the limousine that waits for you and the singer. Flash bulbs pop. Fans scream as the singer comes out of the exit. He waves at the crowd. This seems to make the people even more excited. You quickly guide your client through the cleared path and into the limousine. Suddenly, a man jumps out of the crowd behind you. He angrily shouts something at your client. You instantly react and stop the angry man from hurting the singer.

Your client is safe because of your quick thinking. You are a bodyguard, and danger is your business. Bodyguards are men and women who are paid to risk their lives to protect others. They are people with special skills. This book will take you into the world of bodyguards.

Celebrities, such as rock stars, create a lot of excitement when they go out in public. Sometimes fans get out of control. That's when a celebrity's bodyguard might have to take action.

CHAPTER 1

Serious Business

Bodyguards play an important role in today's world. They do exactly what their job title suggests: They guard a person so that the person will not be physically hurt. There are many different kinds of danger and threats from which bodyguards protect their clients. These threats can include kidnapping, murder, and blackmail. Many people think that bodyguards are simply muscle-bound tough guys like the ones they see in Hollywood movies. In reality, most bodyguards are thoughtful, bright people who take their jobs quite seriously. Professional bodyguards understand the importance of blending in with their surroundings. They make themselves noticed only when it is necessary.

Bodyguards who protect celebrities are careful not to get swept up in the exciting lives of their superstar clients. Instead, they closely watch every person their client comes into contact with.

Good bodyguards are well educated, understand people, and have trained in security techniques. Many bodyguards come from federal law enforcement organizations. These organizations include the U.S. Secret Service, the Central Intelligence Agency (CIA), and the Federal Bureau of Investigation (FBI). People who have served in the military may also make good bodyguards. The military has special groups that offer experience that can be helpful to people who want to be bodyguards. Two examples of these groups are the Navy SEALS and Delta Force.

RISKY BUSINESS

Today, most bodyguards prefer to be called personal protection specialists or executive protection specialists.

The president of the United States has been protected by agents of the U.S. Secret Service since 1901. Just like every other president since then, President George W. Bush (left) never goes anywhere without his Secret Service bodyguard.

Types of Bodyguards

Bodyguards are generally used in four main areas of work. The four areas are government, law enforcement organizations, the military, and the private sector.

Governments all over the world need to protect their leaders and other important officials. They set up

organizations to protect these important people. The U.S. Secret Service is responsible for protecting the president and vice president of the United States and their families. The Secret Service also arranges protection for leaders from other countries who visit the United States. The FBI has its own security team that is used to protect judges, witnesses, and defendants in important court cases. The State Department's Diplomatic Security Service provides security for diplomats, or people who represent the United States in foreign countries.

Law enforcement organizations of state and local governments are usually responsible for protecting governors, mayors, and other important officials. Often, the state police or the public safety department is in charge of arranging and providing this security. In the military, many high-ranking officers are assigned a driver who is also trained to act as a bodyguard. Private-sector bodyguarding includes protecting famous public personalities, celebrities, and business people.

Michael Bloomberg (center), mayor of New York City, always travels with his bodyguards. His bodyguards are made up of officers from the New York City Police Department.

The Samurai played an important role in Japan until the mid-1800s. This photo shows a samurai from the 1860s.

Early Bodyguards

The use of bodyguards goes back to ancient times. Most bodyguards were special groups of soldiers assigned to protect a leader such as an important general, a king, or a queen. For example, in ancient Rome, a special group of soldiers that protected the leaders was called the Praetorian Guard. This group existed in the second century B.C. At first, they were bodyguards for the generals of the Roman army. Then, they became bodyguards for Roman emperors.

In Norway, between 800 and 900 A.D., King Harald Fairhair used a group of warriors known as berserkers as the household guard. The berserkers were very tough warriors.

In Japan, in the eighth century, Japanese warriors called samurai served as bodyguards. The samurai worked for local chiefs called shoguns. Shoguns controlled land and used the samurai to keep them safe and in power.

In 1485, England's Henry VII created the Queen's Body Guard of the Yeomen of the Guard (QBGYG). The QBGYG still exists today, but acts only in special royal and governmental events.

In the United States, the Secret Service was put in charge of the security for the president in the early 1900s. Years later, its responsibilities were widened to include protection of the vice president and other officials.

CHAPTER 2

Prepared for Danger

There are no fixed standards or rules for becoming a bodyguard in the United States. However, many schools and centers offer professional, specialized training to those interested in becoming bodyguards. Bodyguarding attracts men and women from all walks of life. Many bodyguards already have special skills. Some bodyguards once worked for the government in areas of security. Often, others are police officers looking to earn extra money. Also, bodybuilders, martial artists, and boxers often train to be bodyguards. Let's take a closer look at the qualifications of a good bodyguard.

When it comes to defense, bodyguards need to be ready for anything. This is why they study martial arts.

What It Takes

Being able to work in different situations is one of the most valuable qualities a bodyguard can have. For example, sometimes a bodyguard works alone. Other times, several bodyguards work together as a team.

As long as they are on a job, bodyguards never take a vacation from their responsibilities. Above, a Secret Service agent looks out for trouble while President George W. Bush and his father, former president George H. Bush, enjoy some time together fishing.

A bodyguard must be able to take on jobs that may last only a few hours—or as long as several weeks, or even months. He or she also has to be flexible and work by the client's schedule. This might mean working very early in the morning or very late at night.

Bodyguards have to be good at planning ahead. This means looking over a client's schedule to see where he or she is going. Then the bodyguard comes up with a plan to deal with anything that might happen. This important part of a bodyguard's job is called risk assessment of the client. The bodyguard must have good judgement. Risk assessment involves studying every part of the client's life to find possible dangers and threats. Then, the bodyguard must come up with a plan to keep the client from harm.

In Fighting Shape

Bodyguards need to have a clean, neat appearance. Also, they must be in excellent physical condition. They must be able to keep up with their clients, especially if the clients are physically active. Chances are that if a client is going jogging or even jet skiing, his or her bodyguard will too.

Bodyguards need to have a good knowledge of unarmed fighting. Martial arts such as judo and karate provide very helpful skills. A series of well-placed kicks or punches can stop an attacker and allow a bodyguard time to get his or her client to safety.

There are four things that are important to being successful in unarmed combat. First, a bodyguard needs a basic understanding of defensive fighting techniques. Second, he or she must have the physical ability to use those techniques effectively. To be successful at self-defense, a bodyguard needs to have strength, stamina, flexibility, and speed. It is not enough to simply know the right way to block a punch or deliver a kick. The bodyguard must be able to fight back an attacker and stop him or her. Third, a bodyguard must be able to deal with stressful situations. Finally, the bodyguard must have the will to win and not give up.

The Fear Factor

When faced with a life-threatening situation, such as a robber with a gun, most people's first response is fear. Fear warns people that they are facing danger. Sometimes, people freeze up and cannot act in such situations. Bodyguards are taught to put aside their fears and act quickly. A bodyguard is taught to counter-attack with great force when confronted by an attacker. He or she is trained to prevent the attacker from striking again. During an attack, there is a

Though many bodyguards choose not to carry a gun, sometimes they have to. This bodyguard is protecting a government official on a visit to a foreign country.

chance that the bodyguard will get hurt. A bodyguard, however, accepts the possibility of injury as part of the job: The safety of the client comes first.

Carrying Weapons

Many bodyguards carry guns while they're on the job. Their decision to carry a gun is affected by several factors. These factors include concerns about how much danger the client may be facing. Also, the client may have a say in the decision. If a client has children, he or she may not want an armed person around them. In fact, in many cases, having a gun can become a problem. If a bodyguard gets into a fight defending his or her client, he or she could lose control of the gun to the attacker. That makes a bad situation worse.

If a bodyguard does carry a gun, he or she must know how to use it correctly—in any situation. To do this, bodyguards often learn close quarter shooting (CQS). CQS involves situations where the bodyguard is very close to an armed attacker and has very little time to make a decision. An example of this would be a kidnapping at gunpoint. If armed kidnappers are racing toward the bodyguard and his or her client, the

Bodyguards go to special driving schools to learn how to drive in all kinds of unsafe situations.

bodyguard has just a few seconds to decide how to react. CQS teaches bodyguards how to defend a client in this type of situation.

Behind the Wheel

Bodyguards often have to act as drivers for their clients. When that happens, the bodyguards must be up to the job. Special driving schools teach bodyguards how to drive to keep their clients safe. However, the

skills these schools teach are not the kind you'll learn in Driver's Ed! There are three different driving techniques that a bodyguard needs to know: defensive driving, evasive driving, and offensive driving. Defensive driving involves skills that are necessary to avoid accidents that may be caused by other drivers or unsafe road conditions. Evasive driving lessons teaches bodyguards how to keep out of ambushes and other

Driving
Techniques

The following driving techniques are two examples of high-speed reverses. These techniques require special training, so definitely do not try them yourself. One of the most important driving skills a bodyguard must have is being able to do a high-speed reverse. A high-speed reverse is making a fast, emergency stop and then driving backward at top speed. This technique is used to get away from roadblock ambushes.

The J Turn, also called a reverse 180, requires the bodyguard to move the car in reverse at a high speed and then turn the wheel sharply. This causes the car to spin 180 degrees and face the opposite direction. As the front of the car comes around, the bodyguard shifts into drive and races away from danger.

The Bootleg Turn is used when the bodyguard is driving forward and wants to go in the opposite direction. While going forward quickly, the bodyguard turns the wheel and applies the emergency brake. This causes the rear of the car to slide around until the car has done a 180-degree turn. Then, the bodyguard releases the emergency brake and races off.

Many bodyguard training schools teach their students the proper way to handle and shoot their guns.

dangerous situations. In offensive driving, the bodyguard uses his or her vehicle as a weapon. This includes such tactics as ramming the vehicle into the attacker's vehicle to force it off the road. The driving courses usually run for two to five days. The cost of studying at one of these driving schools is not cheap. Many driving schools charge around two thousand dollars for a four-day course.

Training Schools

There are hundreds of schools in the United States that offer bodyguard training. Training schools offer a wide range of subjects that every bodyguard must know. Classes can be as short as one or two days or as long as several weeks. They cover performing emergency medical care, understanding different kinds of security systems, dealing with urban

Two-way radios that allow bodyguards to send and get messages are very important tools used in keeping a client out of danger.

terrorism, and doing advance work. In advance work, a bodyguard studies the place the client is going to visit. The bodyguard then makes the necessary preparations to make the visit safe.

Bodyguards might also learn how to write reports, give orders to others, and use the latest equipment that can be helpful on the job. For example, they learn to use small radios and receivers that allow them to talk with other bodyguards on a team assignment. Taking classes to master these many skills can be expensive. Classes can cost anywhere from two hundred dollars to over three thousand dollars.

Paid to Protect

A bodyguard's salary depends on the bodyguard's experience and the kind of job he or she is hired to do. Some bodyguards work for themselves. Other bodyguards work for security companies that provide bodyguard services. A bodyguard working for a large, successful security company might have a starting salary of about $35,000 a year. He or she might also receive health benefits, vacation time, and overtime pay. After about five years on the job, the bodyguard might be able to earn around $55,000. Generally, the more risk and danger the bodyguard will have to face, the higher his or her salary will be.

CHAPTER 3

Meeting a Client's Needs

Duringhis or her career, a bodyguard will probably work on many different assignments. Some jobs might be high profile. Guarding a movie star is an example of such a job. Other assignments, such as watching over a corporate executive, might be more low key. No matter the situation, a bodyguard will need to know how to deal with his or her client.

Bodyguards to the Stars

Entertainers, politicians, and others in the public eye draw the attention of many people from all over the world. Sometimes, the attention can lead to dangerous

Bodyguards must always dress for success. If they are going to be protecting a business person, a bodyguard has to dress so that he or she will not attract attention and add to the already existing danger.

Thanks to her bodyguards, popstar Shakira continues to rock on — all over the world!

situations. On occasion, someone may stalk a celebrity in a threatening manner. Stalkers may even send threatening letters and make harassing phone calls to the celebrity. Some may go so far as to break into a celebrity's home and attack the celebrity.

The pop singer Shakira was forced to hire bodyguards after receiving death threats. Concern for her safety was so great that a body double was hired to help confuse any would-be attackers. A body double is a person who looks like the celebrity and is used to draw attention away from the celebrity.

Sometimes, the threats to a celebrity are not from a single person but from a dangerous crowd. Pop singer Ricky Martin was almost hurt during a mall appearance in Dallas, Texas. There were eighteen thousand fans on hand—and they all wanted to get close to him. Martin's bodyguards saw that the situation was getting dangerous. They quickly got him out of the mall safely. At the same time, the police pushed back the fans who had gotten out of control.

Sometimes, a celebrity simply wants his or her privacy and does not want to be bothered by TV and newspaper photographers. A bodyguard can help make sure that the celebrity is not harassed. This could mean doing advance work at a restaurant where the celebrity will be eating. The bodyguard would check to see where the exits are located. This is done so the bodyguard can get his or her client out quickly if necessary. Sometimes, photographers will hide in trees near a celebrity's home. The bodyguard would then patrol the grounds of the client's home.

RISKY BUSINESS

When flying on commercial airplanes, the bodyguard should have a seat directly behind the client. If that cannot be arranged, then sitting behind and to the side of the client is acceptable.

Corporate Bodyguards

A lot of bodyguard work is done for businesses, such as financial companies. Working within a company, however, can often be tricky for the bodyguard. Bodyguarding a corporate executive sometimes calls for two teams of bodyguards. One team works the early shift, which is from the time the client leaves for work until the afternoon. Then, another team will come on and stay with the client until late into the evening.

Sometimes two teams will work at once. One team will travel with the client. The second team will go ahead to the client's office. There, the team will make sure that the company's security system has not been tampered with. The team checks with the office's security guards to make sure that there were no problems during the night. They will even check to make sure that all phones and radios are in proper working order.

CHAPTER 4

Bodyguards in Action

Charles Foster is the vice president of the Dream Factory Movie Studio. The studio hasn't had a successful movie in two years. It is losing a lot of money. To cut costs, Foster had to fire five hundred of the studio's fifteen hundred workers. Many workers were very angry about losing their jobs. Since then, he has gotten threatening phone calls and harassing letters at his office and his home. The threats are against him and his family. Foster turned to Advanced Protection Services, a company that offers bodyguarding services, for help.

Hiring a bodyguard is a serious decision. A lot of thought is put into deciding whether or not having a bodyguard is the right thing to do.

Bodyguards not only protect people but their homes and offices, too. Bodyguards use electronic equipment, such as video cameras and monitors, to make sure no one goes where he or she is not allowed.

The Team Takes Charge

Advanced Protection Services sent out a team of eight bodyguards. Rodriguez is the team leader. He has ten years experience as a bodyguard. He also worked fifteen years before that as a U.S. Secret Service agent. The rest of the team is made up of security professionals with different levels of bodyguard experience. All are well trained. There are two women on the team. They are assigned to Foster's wife and daughter. The female bodyguards will be able to offer protection even when Foster's wife and daughter go into a restroom or a dressing room in a mall. When he arrives, Rodriguez turns the pool house into a control center. Video monitors, radios, phones, and other equipment are set up to help the bodyguards keep an eye on the Foster home night and day. Video cameras are set up on all four sides of the house.

Road Rage

The next day, Foster leaves for work. He is accompanied by Rodriguez and four of the bodyguards. The day passes without any trouble. At 6:00 P.M., Foster begins his drive home. Rodriguez is behind the

Making a fast getaway from danger to protect a client is all part of a day's work for a bodyguard.

steering wheel. On a deserted stretch of highway, Rodriguez sees a truck blocking the road. He swings into action. He puts the car into a J Turn. The wheels kick up dirt as they spin in reverse. The car ends up facing the direction it has just come from. Rodriguez slams on the gas pedal. The car shoots down the road, speeding away from the danger.

From a side road, however, another car whips out and sideswipes Foster's car. Rodriguez holds tight to the steering wheel, keeping the car under control.

Since the driver in the other car is not giving up, Rodriguez is forced to take offensive action. He lets the other car get a little ahead of him. Then, he steps on the gas and rams the car that attacked them. The force of the impact sends the other car crashing into a ditch. Rodriguez does not slow down. His responsibility is to get Foster to safety. He speeds to Foster's home. One of the other bodyguards uses his cell phone to call the police. Rodriguez and his team have served their client well.

A Job Well Done

With all the attackers arrested by the police, Foster and his family were out of danger. The bodyguards had done their job well. They protected Foster and his family from danger. They used all the skills they had learned in their training. They faced danger and did not flinch—because being a bodyguard means danger is your business.

Though bodyguards are paid for their work, seeing the client safe is one of the best rewards for a bodyguard.

ambushes (**am**-bush-ez) traps where people hide and then attack someone

avoid (uh-**void**) to prevent something from happening, or to stay away from a person or place

blackmail (**blak**-mayl) the crime of threatening to reveal a secret about someone unless the person pays a sum of money or grants a favor

client (**klye**-uhnt) someone who uses the services of a professional person

defensive (di-**fen**-siv) serving to defend yourself or others

diplomats (**dip**-luh-mats) people who represent their country's government in a foreign country

evasive (i-**vay**-siv) tending to keep away from someone, or to keep out of someone's way

harassing (huh-**rass**-ing) pestering or annoying someone

Praetorian Guard (pree-**tor**-ee-uhn **gard**) soldiers from ancient Rome who protected generals and emperors

professional (pruh-**fesh**-uh-nuhl) a member of a profession, such as bodyguarding; professionals work in fields where special training or study is needed

risk assessment (**risk** uh-**sess**-mehnt) the determining of the possibility of loss or harm to a client

samurai (**sam**-oo-rye) a Japanese warrior who lived in medieval times

sector (**sek**-tur) a part or division of a city or group of people

security (si-**kyoor**-ih-tee) freedom from danger

stalk (**stawk**) to hunt or track a person or an animal in a quiet, secret way

stamina (**stam**-uh-nuh) the energy or strength to keep doing something for a long time

tampered (**tam**-purd) to have interfered with something so that it becomes damaged or broken

techniques (tek-**neeks**) methods or ways of doing something that require skill

threats (**threts**) signs or possibilities that something harmful or dangerous might happen

Abraham, Philip. *The CIA*. Danbury, Connecticut: Children's Press, 2003.

Beyer, Mark. *Secret Service*. Danbury, Connecticut: Children's Press, 2003.

Fine, Jill. *Undercover Agents*. Danbury, Connecticut: Children's Press, 2003.

Goldberg, Jan. *Security Guard*. Philadelphia, PA: Capstone Press, 1999.

Lane, Brian. *Eyewitness: Crime & Detection*. New York: Dorling Kindersley Publishing, 2000.

Meltzer, Milton. *Case Closed: The Real Scoop on Detective Work*. New York: Scholastic Inc., 2001.

Organizations

American Bodyguard Association
7915 South Emerson Avenue, Suite 296
Indianapolis, IN 46237
(800) 220-4876

United States Secret Service
Office of Government Liaison & Public Affairs
950 H Street, Northwest
Suite 8400
Washington, D.C. 20223
(202) 406-5708

Web Sites

The Official United States Secret Service Web site
www.secretservice.gov/index.shtml
This official government Web site tells about the Secret Service's history and mission. Find out where field offices are located and how you can apply to become an agent.

Federal Law Enforcement Training Center
www.fletc.gov
This Web site has information about the training provided by the Federal Law Enforcement Training Center.

About the Author

Heidi Zeigler grew up in Texas. She currently lives and works in Boulder, Colorado, where she writes poetry and nonfiction literature. Heidi is a professor of English at Front Range Community College in Colorado.